Pieces Of Me

By

Samuel Davis Jr.

ISBN: 1-4107-5144-9 (e-book)
ISBN: 1-4107-5143-0 (Paperback)
ISBN: 1-4107-5142-2 (Dust Jacket)

This book is printed on acid free paper.

Library of Congress Control Number: 2003092935

Printed in the United States of America
Bloomington, IN

1stBooks - rev. 05/19/03

Audra, thank you for supporting my project - It is truly a pleasure to know you - We will continue to work together with this law Enforcement thing - Remember - you can trust me!

Dedicated

In memory of:

Viola (Nana) Davis

Sammy (S.M.) Davis

And

Betty Payne

My Family

Table Of Contents

Acknowledgements

I would like to thank God 1st of all, for blessing me with health and strength, along with my understanding of life. Thanks for watching over me. My wife Aimee, who has also helped me to understand life, read and critiqued most every poem I have ever written. My children, Talia, Kamin, and Sammy, I will forever work hard for you all, Daddy loves you very much!! My parents Sam and Cathy, who had developed the blueprint of what organized family life should be, especially my mom who told me to, "never stop writing and to follow this dream!" I will mom, I promise. I love you as well. My brothers and their families, Mike, Tommy, and Gerry- especially Tommy who has inspired several of my poems including, "The Image." I love you Danielle (my little sister) I know you are there, and Glen as well. To my grandparents Charles and Rosie. To my many aunts and uncles, Bobby, Helen, Billy, Walter, Lurlene, Yvonne, Overton, Shelton, Charles Jr, Oneil, (OC), Joyce, Elaine, Christina, Victor, I love you all, you know your nephew is pushing to make you proud. To my many cousins, especially Selena, Joe and the kids. Demont Marrow, (BIG DEE) my other brutha, and Roseanne. Damon and Susanne Mireski and family, thank you because you have always been there for me. To my family at the Sacramento Police Department, especially my pig bowl teammates. Jim Hyde, and Sue Feenstra, thanks for being there for me when my roller coaster was traveling somewhat out of control. It has been repaired!! Ruby River, thanks for the wisdom. Tom Shrum, what can I say, you've been there and been real with all that I've given you to read, thanks. My classmates from 91-BR-01, Dave Peletta, Mitch Marquez, and Michelle Lazark, I love you guys for being so real and not judging me, truly a friendship unconditional. Always on my mind is Rodney Cooper and his family, Donnell Sand, and my friend Bill Bean, I love you guys, and I miss you. Sharon Cadogan, Gino Basso, and Shawn Joyce, I remember your help, thanks. Flosse Crump for my start. Cecil Calender for being my rock...and such a great role model. Much love to anyone that has proofread my material and given constructive criticism, I will be calling on you again in the future so plan on it!! Dani Crawford and Terrel Marsh, Jim Ashley, and Mike

C, from 7-11, especially, My boy Virgil Rogers…hang in there "V" luck will be changing soon, they can never keep a good person down. My Friends at the "Laptop Connection," thank you for you computer expertise, especially you Kao. For the few that have done me wrong, silly fools, you've only made me strong!! And for all that believe in me, thank you!

Introduction

"Pieces of Me," is my first book of poetry. The title's meaning is quite significant in itself, as it relates to my life's journey over the past few years. Following the traditional moreways and folkways in our modern day society I had lived for several years honestly believing that emotions for the most part were to stay bottled inside of me. Because I am a man I could not show my true and honest emotional feelings. To reveal tears, or to show compassion would make me appear weak, at least in modern society's standards. So on the outside, I had built this false front, this cold demeanor, fearing I would be emotionally exposed, but on the inside, because of all that I was experiencing in my life with my family, my job, my past, I could no longer suppress these emotions inside of me. Many days it felt as if my soul was burning up with confusion. I was not being true and real to myself, and it was eating me up.

My walk in life had began to pick up pace that accelerated from a walk to a fast pace jog. I was not keeping up, and was not ready for it. I was raised by both of my parents. They have been married for over forty years. I felt pressure from their situation, as I worked to understand if my relationship with my wife was appearing to me from an oblique perspective. I was the mirror's image of my father who was a very strong male role model for his four sons. I attempted to emulate him when I felt comfortable doing so because this is all that I knew, this is all I've ever seen. I'd watched him and my mother interact for years, so I figured that was how I should be as well. Stern in his ways, no nonsense, which was in direct contradiction with my jovial personality, but I continued to attempt to make the puzzle pieces fit, even though they did not.

The problem as I now realize was, they were old school traditional, and I was married and raising children in the "new school era." Things were not working for me, and I began to erode to a certain degree inside. I did not know what the hell was going on in my life, or in my mind for that matter. The relationships with my three brothers were somewhat rough edged, or strained to say the least. I had begun to experience brief harassment on the job. A job I had been working for over a decade. My several friends began to throw their life's problems on me, and I was to help them, when it was truly me who needed help. I had to answer this certain life challenge, and instead of folding, I reacted as I was raised to. I began to search for an understanding. I also began to fight with my inner strength as well as with my ink pen.

I began to fight off all the adversity I was faced with. A calm arose in my mind, then came my bout with writing poetry. During the initial stretch, I wrote poems to my wife. They were all about her, and they were all about how much I truly loved her. I feared losing her, which caused a great deal of stress during that time. I wrote some forty poems to her within approx three weeks. Can you imagine that? My head was spinning like a hard drive. These poems started off pretty elementary, then they began to pick up depth, and a serious significant meaning along with an understanding of our commitment to one another. She loved them to say the least, it's not often that a man can write his woman meaningful poetry from his heart. I was opening up. I began to address every problem I had through poetry. Writing poetry became therapeutic for me and my head began to clear the more I wrote. Confidence began to re-surface strongly and through my slow but steady progression of comprehending life, I placed myself into a more elevated place. I could not have recovered so quickly if my wife, family and friends did not support me. My wife and I began to get along a great deal better, and in quick time my brothers and I worked on our rough-edged relationships with each other. This worked out well.

I filed away the many problems that bothered me for years and years. I began to write about them, and with me writing poetry, I would get over these issues and I was able to move on from them. I also began to feel so much better inside of my soul. My existence once again appeared to mean something. I was looking at life through a new realistic point of view, I did not sugar coat any situation, nor did I evade anything. However I did determine, either a person is with me or they are not. The ones that weren't were quickly discarded. I had to take better control over my life, so I had to make some serious choices. That was no problem.

As I searched for a term to best describe what was happening to me, I was hit over the head by an anvil. This was my "walk in life." There was no avoiding it; there was no escaping it. I was being challenged by life and the trials and tribulations that come along with it. When I figured out this term, it made things better for me. I went out and bought a bible for added understanding, and strength. I began to read it. During this time more drama appeared. On September 11, 2001, the World Trade Center twin towers were reduced to rubble by terrorist attacks, and the Pentagon was badly damaged. The world was changing, steadfastly, and so was my world. My grandfather passed away five months later. I continued to write poetry during these events and I guess you can say I was in therapy so to speak. Writing has helped me, and in this book are poems about many thoughts and feelings I experienced through my journey within these few years. As I got better in my mind, I often reminisced over past emotional issues. I wrote about them as well. My poetry began to read like a diary and I dated each one of them for my own personal reasons.

I now realize that during my "walk in life," each emotional experience is a piece of who I truly am. "Pieces of Me," is a work of self-expression. I am not about to suppress my emotions ever again in my lifetime. "I am me," and in this book I truly expose my emotional side on several fronts, on several topics.

This is new school. I am new school. I am not afraid of telling the world how much I love my wife or my family. I've been this way for some time but it took this great degree of adversity to confirm these feelings. Most of my friends have always classified me as "real." They just have no idea how far I've walked to get here, but I am truly here now.

The constant positive entity during these trials and tribulations of my life was and still is my mother, Mrs. Cathy Davis. Regardless of the drama, she kept a cool head and thought pattern for me. I know where I get my calm resolve. This woman supported every endeavor I have ever had to deal with, and I personally feel that she is one of the main inspirations for this book. No doubt she deserves her own paragraph in my first book. Thank you mom.

I hope you enjoy reading about these pieces of my life. Each and every piece like a puzzle has completely assembled me. Life is about learning and growing, I am constantly doing both. I hope you can identify with me.

Enjoy my book.

SD

Sam Davis

Forward

Reality and its significance

What does "real" mean as this word pertains to experiencing life and life's walk? Is being real, or reality different for everyone, or is it the same for us all? It appears to me that because each and every one of us have experiences that differ in life, our realities on a large scale will differ as well. However the word "reality, which may be seen differently through the eyes of others, basically has a duel meaning. These meanings to me are "what is real, or what is true."

We dance around reality quite often hoping to evade it, one would guess, but as we do this, and we all do it, we don't realize that evasion of what is "real," or the evasion of the truth, is only living a lie, or perhaps a fantasy that only exists in our minds. And once we get to this point we are completely out of touch with what is "real," and what is "true." The significance of accepting reality, or accepting the truth is, you will be real and true to yourself as well as others, instead of a fantasy that lives inside of the mind.

Why are we so afraid to deal with reality?

Why are we so afraid to deal with the truth?

Are we ashamed that in some way our deep feelings and fears will be exposed? Or maybe we fear that others will learn our flaws, as if we are the only ones that have flaws. The thought of fear will keep many of us from being "real and true," to ourselves as well as "real and true to others."

Why wouldn't a man tell his wife how much he loves her?

Why wouldn't a man allow a male friend of his to know how much he loves his wife if they were to ever get into this conversation?

Mainly because of the fear of being made to look soft, weak, or spineless in the eyes of others. The man or men that live in this fashion in this here example may know how he feels inside, but since he doesn't verbally express to his wife how he truly feels about her, nor would he ever tell any of his friends how giddy he still is about his wife, he lives somewhat reclusive and will never deal with the truth of how he feels about his wife, at least to her and others. He may acknowledge love in his own mind, but not on the outside.

"Pieces of Me," in my opinion shatters this way of thinking. In this book I am completely real about my feelings. I hide nothing. My walk in life has carried me to this point. I have been, and continue to be a student of life, and one of my classes is self-honesty, or self-truth, aka "what is real, or reality." There is no need of holding back. I do not fear what people think about me, as long as I know that I am being completely "real" and honest about myself. This is me, so like it or not, this is what you get.

I completely expose myself in this book hoping to touch the reader from a "realistic" and truthful perspective. Again, I will never be afraid of what people will think about me. As my poem "Reflection," suggests. "Are you satisfied with the image the mirror reflects?" Well...are you?

At this point in my life, I am.

This is why in my opinion reality is so significant. At days end you must be able to look at yourself in the mirror, and be satisfied with what you see. You are, or you aren't; only you know the answer to that.

When you read "Pieces of Me," think of your life, as it really is, not some fantasy-like Utopia. If you do this you should be able to embrace with my emotions and have a better understanding of who you are, which may lead to you coming to terms with your life's walk. It's o.k. to show your emotions.

By no way am I saying that I am completely problem or issue free, but I'm in a different place in my life now, and I find it a great deal easier to deal with life's peaks and valleys.

That Hurtful Day

(inspired by the events of 9-11)

Another year, Another thought.
A hurtful day,
the sadness it brought.

Children without their fathers, forced to be raised this way.
Mothers without answers for them,
forced to relive that hurtful day.

Husbands facing the same predicament, raising children without their
wives,
having to painfully explain to them,
why their mothers had lost their lives.

A nation…watching. An event beyond belief,
left hoping to get over this hurtful day,
which had caused us so much grief.

The endless quest to understand, the gray clouds filled with rain,
the multitude of emotions,
necessary to ease our pain.

We are all Americans. Not a difficult thing to see,
an attack against our country,
is an attack on you and me.

Bow your heads for these families. Silently say a prayer.
They deserve this moment we're giving them,
let them know how much we care.

Sam Davis
9-11-02

1

Sail Away

I'm mostly over the negative,
feelings I've carried inside.
Once muddled with issues it now appears,
their washing away with the tide.

Sail away,
burdensome past.
Your time to visit is over,
happiness has come to last.

I didn't enjoy even a minute of your arrival,
let alone your stay.
Showing up uninvited with your cloudy murk,
wrecking my sunny days.

So sail away,
deep into the abyss of the sunset.
The time has come for happiness to visit,
and for you, it's time to forget.

Sam Davis
7-26-02

From Day One

With my mouth wide open, I stood there staring,
at this awesome view. Existing in a dream like state,
glaring into the thought of only you.

So deeply snared by your beauty,
my soul began elevating.
My heart began pumping wildly, my existing thoughts, precipitating.

How rare the possibility, but this just might,
be what we know as love at 1st sight

I touch your hand as we shook,
and I remained so captivated by your look.
My feet firmly cemented, I could not move,
constantly praying nothing would disturb this groove.

Days, months and years have passed since that day,
reminiscing is so much fun.
But I know now just as I did back then,
I've loved you from day one.

Samuel Davis Jr.
12-19-02

Destination Unknown

Is it my quest to be alone?
Am I orbiting space,
searching for a place to call home?

I often stress on how the things I touch somehow,
turn to stone, so many miles ahead of me,
before I reach my throne.
What the hell am I doing wrong?

I try and listen to the advice I've been given,
hoping the words will somehow glisten,
and assist my comprehension.
No such luck though, I end up with only failure to show.

Am I taking the correct route,
to work on my life, to figure life out?
Maybe, but maybe not, my water boiling over,
temperature is far too hot.

Trying to figure out life can be quite demanding,
along with my learnings, I pray for understanding.

Sam Davis
12-12-02

4

The Book

My books cover is so worn.
The edges of many of its pages are tattered.

My book cannot be compared to the average textbook,
because it is so much more resourceful.

Though worn, its cover stays intact.
Even with the tattered edges, its pages can be clearly read.

It's story…well its worth reading over and over again.
Because within these tattered pages
are my life's experiences.

I read from them daily and from time to time,
new pages are added.

One day the new pages will too become tattered,
but will also be clearly read.

With life comes learning, and as long as the cover stays intact,
I will never lose its pages.

Sam Davis
08-17-02

Detachment

The sensational flow of negativity,
escorts a feeling that I am secondary.
No longer am I primary, infact I appear quite ordinary.

There was a time I felt so connected with you, a time I felt so
protected with you.
The winds of uncertainty have left me disconnected,
my entire existence is being tested.

The stressful times that we have endured over the years,
have come back to visit me and reproduced tears.
The memories echo loudly of these times, loud bells ringing, a
deafening chime.

From the real world my soul has temporarily disconnected,
amplifying this feeling that is far less than protected.
My ego crushed left feeling rejected, my significance hypothetical,
appearing neglected.

I am mysterious to even myself.
It's these times I must place this depression on its shelf.
I'm feeling sorry for myself on this day, and deeply hoping not to
waste away.

Reentering the real world is soon becoming my focus,
moving on from the past is simply a must.

Sam Davis
09-20-02

Their Talking

They throw stones. Not literally,
but with verbal tones, attempting to get my goat.
Constantly pulling my chain and,
bringing down rain, when my forecast is sunny.

They don't know me, but on me they speak,
and their sentiment reeks, of loneliness, insecurity and instability.

Living in glass houses, which they are truly encased,
providing all this gossip that spreads with rapid pace.
So much work just to put me down, the backstabbing conversations
occurring when I'm not around.

But I am wise to each and every one of you guys.
There's been no surprise to your existence or your lies.
You've been exposed in this lifestyle that you chose,
throwing stones wrapped in verbal tones,
isn't it only obvious why you are so alone?

Sam Davis
09-30-02

Rhythmic

It took some time, but now I know,
the power of the constant pulsating flow
of our existence together.

The sensual guide, steady.
Like the rise of the tide, ready
for the minute we embrace, and come face to face.

The lost stares into your eyes.
The strength of our ties,
Rhythmic, is this euphoric feeling.
Orgasmic, as it sends me reeling.

The emotional feeling of love, is gigantic
while we experience these moments, climactic.

Rhythmic, as our hearts thump wildly, racing.
While our souls dance proudly, chasing
intimacy in its most awesome form.
A meeting destined since the day we were born.

Sam Davis
10-01-02

Friends

I thought my absence in these years,
may have helped me avoid the tears, and the fears
of acknowledging that you are no longer here, with us.

But I was wrong, because I returned,
and it was obvious that you were gone. I seemed so alone,
as I visited your home.

I can still hear your voice and if given the choice,
of course I'd want to hear it daily.

My friend…the thought of you being gone is a hurtful one,
that seems so wrong. Though we are all forced now to move on,
we search for answers that will make us strong.

I shall cherish the thought of the time we spent.
The love you brought the places we went.
Our memories continue to live inside of me, such histories,
are a blueprint and are so key, to living an eternal friendship,
forever friends,
a deeper kinship.

Sam Davis
10-06-02

Hope

If observing life, one honestly can conceive,
that sometimes life is plain unfair.
It's through hard times we learn a sense of hope,
but at time hope's existence seems rare.

Though hope seems invisible,
when times get really rough.
A glimmer of faith is what I need, to
make those matters seem less tough.

I must place hope in my arms, and never lose it,
holding it firmly each day.
Because if I lose it, my desires will follow,
and my soul will fade away.

So, if observing life, one can also conceive, although
sometimes unfair, life is simplistic to maintain,
place hope in your arms, and never lose it,
it's use helps to ease the pain.

Sam Davis
9-3-01

On The Outside

I'm labeled controversial
by some that I know.
But I think that's because,
of the distant presence that I show.

Either you know me,
or you don't.
It's my option to let you inside of me,
either I'll trust you or I won't.

Maybe it's because I stand fearless,
to those that many of my friends fear.
My life's walk has taught me to be courageous,
with the will to persevere.

I'm blessed with the mentality of a warrior.
Knowledge, confidence, and wisdom contributing to my pride.
those attributes forever supporting my success and,
act as a shield carried by my side.

No, see I am not controversial.
If this is your opinion, you don't know me well.
You will never see inside of me,
only the outside hardened shell.

My somewhat misleading mask.

S. Davis
2001

The Balance

When the teeter-totter of life has you dejected,
emotionally soaring out of control,
It's now my time to show you direction,
There's a depth of loving wisdom in my soul.

I will answer all of your desires,
tell me what you need.
Constantly balancing your position to make you whole,
There is nothing that I can't achieve.

I fight the worrisome task of,
leveling off several of your emotions.
Extremely difficult at times I continue to battle,
what is fluid like the stir of the ocean.

No matter how drastically the scales may tip,
where your emotions are concerned.
My love for you will reset that scale,
and the balance will return.

By Sam Davis
2001

Pieces

As like the eyes of the house fly,
there's a thousand images of me.
Inside each and every image,
is so much more for these eyes to see.

My life is very complex to understand.
One thousand facets to undergo.
But life itself becomes very complex and confusing,
bottled emotions, I'm hoping they won't show.

At times I can't concentrate, can't clearly see,
when so many eyes are opened wide,
trust in myself is all I can do,
to better how I feel inside.

One thousand eyes see one thousand scenarios,
many I deal with from day to day.
Even when some of the eyes are closed, so many stay open,
and mass confusion comes out to play.

These are all pieces of me, and these
fragments of my life take their toll.
One day I know I can close these eyes,
I only pray this will rest my soul.

Sam Davis
2001

A Must

The house in which I live,
is see through, somewhat transparent,
but only to one...the almighty,
Dear Lord, am I that apparent.

My past sins—countless.
Most have come to pass,
others I must work on,
while taking refuge in my house of glass.

Help me Lord to understand,
my life and to find my way,
through the brush, help me find prosperity,
life's confusing, my wires frayed.

It's important that I comprehend, your word,
I must be able to see.
I want and need your guidance or,
this glass house will crash down on me.

Sam Davis
9-17-01

14

This Falling Feeling

Somberesque and somewhat concerned,
a waning comprehension and feeling.
Victimized by this emotion called love.
Once hard, my surface…now peeling.

I've feared this feeling,
for quite some time.
Prolonging the inevitable,
because love isn't always kind.

Once wrapped comfortably,
an insulated body with my soul enclosed.
I now live terrified, as I fear,
my heart has been left exposed.

I'm apprehensive to trust,
this is where I firmly stand.
To fully open up to true love,
I don't know if I honestly can.

The time is now, although,
I may not want it, I really must give it a try.
I don't want to live the rest of my life,
wondering if I missed out…and why.

Sam Davis
9-10-01

Our Time

A mad dash to escape what we know,
as reality.

Is the feeling I experience when you are,
in my arms.

I'd ask that time would comfort us and stand still.
Allowing much for us to share in our,
dream world.

Maybe not forever, but for just a few minutes then.
A suspended measure of lastingness.

No music, no surrounding noise,
no children.

Just you and I, in our dream world together,
without a clock or the concept of time.

Sam Davis
2001

As A Man

As a man, I have learned…
To stand firm and to diligently fight my own battles.
But…to choose these battles carefully before fighting them.
As a man I have learned…
Never to back down while fighting these battles and to remain
fearless regardless of the possible circumstances…
ultimately finishing every battle victorious.
As a man I have learned…
To be a student of life, reading and comprehending each day as if it
were a textbook.
As a man I have learned…
Trust the trustworthy, and aggressively discard those who are not!
As a man I have learned…
To love my family unconditionally, flaws included.
Treat my wife with the same respect I'd give my mother and…
to raise my children as I was once raised.
As a man I have learned…
That God is #1, followed by my family, then friends.
As a man I have learned…
To look for acceptance from me and me only—period!
As a man I have learned so much,
a continual quest for life's blueprint.

Samuel Davis Jr.
8-9-01

Driftwood

So many issues wash in with the tide.
Hanging around taunting me, forcing me to choose a side.

I must decide to clean it up now or deal with it later,
But more debris may wash in if I wait, somehow I must cater.

The driftwood of issues are gathering. Pile by pile, pound by pound.
Because of my reluctance, the piles have become larger—such a
burden to clear this mound.

Fragments of driftwood—skeletal remains of the past—
A shipwreck of emotions, foundations shattered with the crash.

Reminiscent of my own issues, which I have dealt with the best I
could.
These skeletal structures now crashed and crumbled, pose as this
driftwood.

I know it's inevitable, the results of my decision,
To continue to contemplate, or to cleanup with major precision.

Sam Davis
06-21-02

Decaying Existence

Running from the issues in your past,
at a pace extremely fast.
Searching for satisfaction,
knowing the running cannot last.

Yet all outside advice falls on deaf ears,
and it appears you will continue
to drown in a sea of your own tears.

Far too stubborn for your own good,
the decaying of your existence,
is rapid, like rotting wood.

The inevitable fate of one that does not learn,
is failure, regardless of which direction you may turn.
You are welcoming a future filled with much pain,
a suffering existence consumed by flames.

Sam Davis
12-08-02

The Fight or Flight of Loves Power

Some scurry away while others traipse in.
Some hoping to avoid it, others are searching within.

The Power of Love can make one flee. Yet others run towards it's direction.
Many have been injured by Love's power, others pray for it's protection.

The hurt one knows it takes hard work and just aren't willing to give the time.
"Not worth the effort," they say to themselves, hoping two hearts would align.

Some of us stay optimistic, having a positive future in mind.
Being alone for very long, they're willing to sacrifice time.

"Inspiriting" they must stay if they hope to wear love's crown.
The other choice is to be pessimistic and bitterly wear a frown.

At some point in your life, the Power of Love will reach towards you.
Optimistic or Pessimistic you must ask yourself, "What if anything will I do?"

Either embrace Love with open arms and gallantly take a chance.
Or turn away cowardly and miss the invite to Love's dance.

Sam Davis
06-14-02

I'm Out

I'm leaving it all behind.
Turning over a new leaf.
No longer concerned about past drama,
and how it's caused me grief.

I've been down in spirits,
for such a long time.
Worried so much about the feelings of others,
rarely paying attention to mine.

I have walked the tight rope
of what I know as sanity.
No more will I try to balance these feelings,
and try to save humanity.

I'm washing my hands
of this negative energy,
that many have thrown my way.
Showing no compassion for me.

So if you plan to talk with me later,
about your issues, hoping that I'd care.
Don't stop off where I lived yesterday,
Because I will not be there!

Sam Davis
07-12-02

The Crutch

Who am I?
Obviously the scapegoat,
used as the catalyst, to mule the issues meant for others to tote.

A toxic dumping ground overflowing with psychological waste, all
discarded onto me. I'm left with a horrendous taste.

An unwillingness to trust now, and to many I've grown so leery.
Being labeled the "goat" for such a long time my mind has grown
quite weary.

However this was yesterday as today has become brand new.
No longer am I going to absorb their needs, they must figure on what
to do.

Playing on my soft side.
Those guilty of this should now walk gingerly, you've raised an
enormous tide.

I'll be here to advise and to listen, but no longer will I work as the
mule.
Handle your business, it's what's best for you, and my advice can
work as your tool.

Sam Davis
06-23-02

Burning

Could someone please just be so kind,
and extinguish these fires in my mind?

Could someone stop the blaze I'm seeing?
My body feels hot,
I'm rapidly breathing. The times come for me to be fleeing.

This "five alarm" fire is out of control.
The burning issues which I harbor inside,
conveniently taken toll.

"So how will it end?" I curiously ask,
with this fire hardly contained.
The consumption of anger will lead to my demise,
a plane crash and burning remains.

Sam Davis
06-16-02

The Image

Confused by the image,
of what I saw as real.
Perfectly seeing a shining object,
when it was dull and lacked appeal.

The image seemed God-like—
Herculean, mighty, strong.
So untouchable was this image,
I never feared it could be wrong.

A voice calling out echoed loudly one day.
Several times the voice said to me.
"Take a closer look at this image,"
It is different from what you see.

"Judge it for what it is,
not what you want it to be.
Because this image was only a mirage,"
·Suddenly devastated, I began to see.

All this time I saw with closed eyes,
reality is what I thought I was seeing.
But the most important lesson I learned from it all,
this image was an ordinary human being.

Sam Davis
9-5-01

All About You

Selfishness,

A quality at times you tend to embrace.
It's all about you when you invite me here,
to your own little private place.

When I enter this room, where only you exist,
my body's present, though transparent,
it has vanished amongst the mist.

My significance appears non-existent,
as I feel my way through the mist.
Whatever problems **I** have **I** leave behind,
not a priority on your list.

I guess I'll wait outside this room,
at times the mist can thicken.
The time spent here can really be explosive,
a bomb that is constantly tickin'.

To avoid the explosion today,
again, I will wait outside this place,
where you hang out when it's all about you,
this thick and misty, self absorbed space.

Sam Davis
06-16-02

Adverse

Adversity...

How you deal with it is essential to your survival.
Some choose to flee. They run, they attempt to hide from it,
scared as if the boogeyman is wide awake underneath
the bed they sleep in, or maybe lurking around the corner
their walking towards.

Those who survive adversity, face it and welcome it's challenge,
and deal with it because they are aware...it's inevitable.

I am a soldier to this inevitable nag, daring the uprising of it's
challenge.
All the while, my mind stays alert.
I counter-punch it as soon as it throws it's first blow.

In the end I will survive it, and then...
well, there is always tomorrow,
a reminder of today.

Sam Davis
2001

What quitters do

Stressed and mentally challenged to
the maximum limit,
One faces a crossroads so to speak.
It is at that moment the decision has
to be made; Do I go on, or do I quit?

The one that quits must face their decision.
It must hurt a person, tremendously inside
to exhibit a lack of effort, a lack of desire, a lack of self-pride.
Yet they must live with their decision to quit.

It takes no effort to complete this task.
When time and circumstances
become difficult is when this person will
wilt, finding the easiest way out of their situation.

So what do quitters do?
It's quite simple.
They fail to succeed.

Sam Davis
2001

My True Calling

So much time we spent together,
the many stories that we've shared.
Becoming friends is how we started,
with subtle hints that we both cared.

Once considered important,
the bright shiny items I would chase.
Suddenly those things meant less and less to me
And quickly, you took their place.

I began to want you around me, entirely
because I felt so comfortable with you there.
I was truly experiencing young love,
with all that time we shared.

Over the years I've come to understand,
this was love and I've continued the falling.
Blessed from the time you've entered my life,
this was my true calling.

Sam Davis
2001

The Black Mood

A quiet and perplexed like
state of being.
Futile attempts to ward off my confusion,
my soul partial to fleeing.

It's unknown where I will run to, insecurely thinking,
I now have growing doubts.
A mission seemingly impossible to fight,
so I search for close escape routes.

This pitch-black environment I securely sit inside of,
grows darker…I can't hear the voices that call.
I am unsure if it's a room that I occupy,
because I cannot even touch it's walls.

So unsure of this eerie side of life's cruel test.
It's boundaries seemingly endless, so wide,
Constantly I fight harder,
with this emotionally stressful ride.

The darkness I sit in,
may only exist in my mind.
I pray to understand these surroundings,
hoping the sun will rise.

Sam Davis
9-8-01

Growing Together

Many years ago we met each other.
With hard work an understanding we are still intact.
It's because we continue to grow together,
and have the wisdom to interact.

Every relationship has it's obstacles to overcome,
and our love is no exception.
Yet, at each stage of our relationship we've continued to grow,
giving our love this prominent protection.

Although we have rarely mentioned it,
we have managed to stay in sync,
bonding together every step of the way,
a natural loving instinct.

We must continue to grow together,
somehow we have done this from the start.
Because growing in different directions, or not at all
will only force us apart.

Sam Davis
2001

Piece by Piece

A fully constructed puzzle, neatly put together.
Though it took years to assemble,
it cannot stay intact forever.

Time will erode this beautiful work of art.
Slowly the pieces will begin to part.
Without a frame, it hangs on a wall, piece by piece it will begin to
fall.

Such is life,
with much strife we put our lives together.
Building a sturdy foundation, a variety of storms to weather.

Once our lives are constructed, we display them. They do stand bold.
Hopefully we've met our life's goals, because in time we will grow
old.
Eventually comes the inevitable descend,
the erosion of the puzzle pieces.
Once they've all fallen, life comes to an end.

Sam Davis
12-10-02

Perfectly Encased

Perfectly encased in a world of our own.
Set aside from the misplaced ones that face the tones, of living in the
real world.
You and I live here alone.

They deal with life on a daily basis, experiencing life and it's many
faces.
There is so much change and a wide range of issues for them to
endure.

But for you and I, our existence is more protected and pure.

It's a love that's untouchable, placed on a shelf,
and for most unreachable. With not even a fall from the shelf,
do we become breakable. No drama, no stress, firmly standing
positive,
and will endure through all of life's tests.

Because we are a memory, and we exist in the mind, with thoughts of,
"what if" which we find quite fine.
Perfectly encased away from life's everyday woes,
Just you and I in our little snow globe.

Sam Davis
11-20-02

Lost Angels

They are honest and innocent minded, though many times
blinded by what they don't know or see,
just how deceiving human beings can be.

The closest thing to angels we have here on earth.
It appears that we often underestimate their worth,
and this angelic gift they've been given at the time of their birth.

Sadly, we will corrupt them, badly,
as they learn the ways of the world.
The passage of days will confuse them after their arrival,
as they learn our morals and values of survival.

They will become less and less angelic then,
and definitely more of a human being.
So much promise is what birth brings, yet
such a short life for these lost angels without wings.

Sam Davis
10-30-02

My Oldest Child

I am somewhat marveled as I reflect on the day
that my oldest child was born.
I became a dad that day, my wife, a mom,
anticipating all this had us completely worn.

The effort your mom put forth on that day,
working so hard to bring you here.
Not in a thousand years could we have imagined
that such a beautiful child would appear.

I stood motionless as I watched your infant body
being taken from your mother.
Your mom and I grew closer that day,
as proud parents we could only stare at one another.

"Look at what we've made," I thought to myself,
your beauty beyond compare.
Look at this angel God has placed into our lives,
knowing we had plenty of love to share.

With your mom resting now, I went to your room,
which was warm and filled with light.
I stood over you, said a prayer to the Lord,
then uttered, "I love you, sleep tight."

Sam Davis
2001

Imani

On this cool September day,
you came along and washed my fears away.

At this time in my life I had somehow lost my way,
I was living a life which had become so uncertain,
until your birth on that September day.

With your birth, I was given new life,
and a new sense of worth.

As in your name "Imani" meaning faith,
I know I have that now,
as I've sampled it's awesome taste.

"How beautiful" you were as I thought to myself,
another child to love and protect. I never imagined as I held you in
my arms,
that we would give birth to a child so perfect.

Sam Davis
11-14-02

In Him I See Me

The smile of this boy,
nearly melts my heart.
From the day of your arrival,
true love from the start.

He runs around the house,
with loads of joy and energy,
he doesn't realize it now,
but in him, I see me.

My little boy,
named after me.
Feeling how I used to feel,
and being like I used to be.

I must continue to work hard,
and give him the life I once had.
Forever sacrificing all for him,
making him proud that I'm his dad.

Sam Davis
2001

Nature's Progression

What happened to the seventeen year old teenager that I once knew?
The young lady I fell in love with, within a week or two.

What happened to the twenty year old pregnant with our first child?
Standing out so beautiful back then, a lone orchid in the wild.

What happened to the young lady appearing at times confused with
not much to say?
Now she glows with confidence, showing wisdom beyond her days.

What happened to the twenty-five year old that always needed me?
Now treading water on her own, swimming in her own liberty.

What happened to the twenty-six year old that gave birth to our other
two children?
The mask of a mother is now what she wears, her confidence so
strong and building.

That teenager I fell in love with, that orchid in the wild,
Has really come into her own, and is no longer a child.

The beauty you possess now, truly unique from your former years.
I am so proud of the woman you've become, it's hard to fight back
tears.

The seventeen year old has somewhat vanished, and so has the
twenty-year old.
Replaced by a woman that knows what she wants, now standing more
solid, more bold.

It's because of this progress that our love blossoms from day to day.
You're my wife and I love you is all I can say, you've helped my find
my way.

Sam Davis
06-06-02

My Tropical Paradise

I'd like to escape to a tropical paradise. Free of daily drama and the
other bullshit,
That tends to encompass my life at times, challenging my wit.

Palm trees, the tan of the sand, with the background of watery blue, is
where I need to be.
Hanging out in my paradise, no one there but me.

My personality is a caring one. I care for others; it's just that plain.
The problem is, they feed off this, and it causes me great pain.

Their problems become my problems dealing with their issues, even
though I have my own.
Their issues have taken the forefront, and to them my feelings aren't
known.

I feel myself free falling, trying to make heads and tails,
Of the shit they are experiencing, a train traveling without rails.

I need my tropical paradise, even if it's in my mind.
A time to shut out the daily drama, sweet paradise it's one of a kind.

Sam Davis
06-09-02

The Writer

Who is the writer of my story?
Am I truly doing the writing,
or does fate claim the glory?

Who is assuring me that I will succeed?
Did I place myself in this position,
or has fate done this deed?

Weird, because I know this story is about me,
but how much do I honestly control,
fate uses its own eyes to see.

And how will fate write my ending?
Will I suffer tales of a broken heart,
tales of a heart not mending?

I must become the sole writer of my story.
I cannot allow fate to claim the glory.
Only I, must place myself into position to succeed.
I can't sit by idle and hope fate does this deed.

Fate can assist me in my endeavors to succeed,
but it must follow me, as I lead.

Sam Davis
03-13-03

One Of Those Days

Have you ever had one of those days,
when it seems impossible to find balance?
You float blindly sifting through a rats maze.

Not a thing goes right these days,
and it seems my fighting ways,
have been snatched from underneath,
missing beyond belief, buried within this grief.

Ill-fate on these days appear,
to follow me closely from the rear.
Waiting for a chance to violently push,
me into its own form of ambush.

These days,
rain clouds following, filled with grays.
Such negativity this day has portrayed,
the loud hopeless message it all has conveyed.

Tomorrow can't get here soon enough.

Sam Davis
1-17-03

My Everything

I step away from my soul, and temporarily abandon my existence.
I can clearly see it all, charting my success from a not so far distance.
Some times have been good, some others have not, but they appear to
carry a common theme.
All of my adult life has been spent with you,
and you are my everything.

There is no me without the presence of you, by my side.
Lord, what would I do, without you, my joy, and my pride?
To whom would I love and confide, without you there as my bride?

My accomplishments are your accomplishments as well,
helping me build confidence, gone, is the fear that I can fail.

Who would have known when you came along,
you would help a strong man, become more strong?
I am what you've helped me become.
You're such an instrumental portion of my success, and then some.

So as we spend the rest of our lives together as King and Queen,
remember, you are the most wonderful person that I have ever seen.
Without you, I would not be me,
you are my everything.

Sam Davis
02-05-03

The Reflection

Are you satisfied with the image the mirror reflects?
Or is reality what you choose to protect?
Only you know what you see.
Is it truly you, or only what you pretend to be?

The image of the mirrors reflection,
if observed honestly will not offer any protection.
It will tell you no lies,
and will dare you to look into your own eyes.

The image is real,
and until you can visit face to face,
the concept of reality,
is one you can't embrace.

Sam Davis
02-14-03

The Realization

I've come face to face with this place in my heart.
Though a tumultuous journey,
I've traveled so many miles from my start.

I've walked this beaten path, optimistically,
even though the negative lurked, forcing me to question my chemistry.

This redwood forest of trees, for such a long time had blocked my view.
Born was the emergence of depth and wisdom. Clearing a path for me,
and I walked through.

So this is where I am.
Cherishing my new place.
Having battled the negative ambiance,
and finding the positive to embrace.

Sam Davis
02-28-03

The Purfect Purson

Oh how we obsess in our search for the, "purfect."
The purfect setting, the purfect plan,
sensing the purfect woman or the purfect man.

We delve for 100 % purfection, as if 90% or 80%,
is such a bad thing.
The simple thought escapes us, No one is purfect.
A guarantee we know that life brings.

Inside our hearts we know there is no purfect purson,
yet we search for them and our outlook on love may worsen.

Such a hypocritical stand we take, looking for this invisible myth,
as our hearts wear down and break.
How do we avoid placing ourselves in this spot?
Hoping for the purfect to come along,
knowing that especially **we** are not.

Our expectations can be so unreasonable.
A purfect purson: so far from feasible.
We must realize there is no purfect prize.
It's for each of us to figure out on our own.
Because thinking that the purfect purson is out there,
may mean a lifetime that you will spend alone.

Sam Davis
03-02-03

A Different Place

I know that many have come to visit me.
I must apologize because I've been gone.
Evaporating from where I was, to where I am now,
traveling within this journey I'm on.

I've learned the significance of my existence.
Arriving in a different place from yesterday,
it took hard work but I've been very persistent.

I am a proud husband and father,
my family has carried me here,
to this place which is so far serene, a place
where they've lessened all of my fears.

My wife, bless her heart,
has helped me to understand the meaning of true love.
Now free of any of the doubts love brings,
I've taken flight like the dove.

My children, they keep me young,
they grow and so many things are key,
to their survival in this world,
a great deal will be taught by me.

That confusing place where I lived yesterday,
is not where I currently reside.
I've finally arrived at a place called home,
with my wife and children inside.

Sam Davis
03-08-03

Thoughts Linger

One year removed from past doubtfulness,
presently attempting to escape its confusing cloudiness.
At times I am finding it difficult to do so,
my mind is playing these tricks on me, I know these thoughts must
go.

Last year's emptiness lurks closely by,
although I'm past the situations,
my soul is reminded and it cries.
Wondering all over again, "why."

The grass still smells the same,
a stimulated reminder of the pain.
The blossoming trees, preparing to grow leaves,
last years' thoughts stay surfaced, I begin to grieve.

Yes, it's the same time of year,
and also surfacing is a lessoned fear.
Mostly not believing that last year will be re-born,
or my poor soul being abandoned, ripped, torn.

But today is not last year.
All day long I've not shed a single tear.
So truly what is my fear?
Today is today, but just in case, I'll drop to my knees and pray.

Sam Davis
03-08-03

Selena

My darling cousin,

So many years have passed us.
You've always been there for me.
Don't ever think that I will forget,
the importance of our history.

I've always considered you as my sister,
one I've always placed so high,
on top of this pedastol,
we will always have that tie.

We are both parents now,
and I know it may seem as though I have forgot,
about the times we spent together as kids,
please believe me, I have not.

I want you to truly know,
how much I love you, though at times it may not show.
Believe me, you are always on my mind.

You will always be,
so very special to me.
I miss you, and I love you.

From your big brother,

Mickey

Sam Davis
1-16-03

Make The Change

The great melting pot we live in,
does not always have the perfect blend.
It is our responsibility to make this mesh,
and help make our country truly the best.

Many cultures surround us,
such a variety of skin tones around us.
With this variety come the unknown,
and because we don't know, unless we get closer as a people,
we can't grow.

So help us make the change.
Shatter the stereotypes that still remain.
Getting to know each other will solve much pain,
you and I together working to achieve this gain.

It will take much work, but in the end,
we will experience the perfect blend.

Samuel Davis Jr.
11-27-02

It Starts Here

My heart is with you.
As your friend I am extremely true.
Non-judgmental, truly honoring our friendship,
as unconditional.

Yet, I feel there is much pain inside of you.
Pain that you are afraid to claim, as your own.
But this pain is truly yours to deal with…
one wrong move and all can be blown.

How do I help you deal with it,
without making you feel uncomfortable about this shit?
Dear friend, you must deal with your past issues,
or they will lead to your end.

You are such a beautiful person inside and out,
but like it or not, allowing past issues to run your life,
your beauty inside and out, will rot.

Decaying away slowly,
your soul will never find its way and will be solely good to no one.
Don't allow your past to last in your mind, body, or soul.
Free yourself of these demons, believe me, they are taking a toll.

Sam Davis
12-02-02

Secret Gone

The doorbell is ringing, who's there?
it's not who you're thinking.
There is a figure on your doorstep,
unless you let it in, its helpful words will be difficult to interpret.

A figure that knows you well,
it wants to help when you choose to dwell.
I've heard it knocks only once, but now it's coming to set you free.
Take advantage of Mr. Opportunity.

Ever feel like a cowboy unable to lasso its steer,
working so diligently to capture life while trying to fight off fear…
You're missing…constantly…badly.

Deep inside, I know this is you,
regardless of the times you say it's untrue.
Your plans to be happy have mostly come up short,
because of the countless missions you do not abort.

Stop fighting what's inevitable, as the driftwood stacks.
Like wild animals,
the past can leave animal tracks.

Sam Davis
12-03-02

The Positive Spin

What do you do when a best friend,
shelters the truth from you, choosing to keep it bottled within?
How do you call them on it?
Do I await the arrival of the positive spin?

For years I have laid idle, yet I wonder why,
I identify all of the tears, even when she does not cry.
Why do I take this stance?,
she becomes the victim and past skeletons begin to prance.

I feel derelict in my duties as her friend.
It remains unknown why I don't speak up,
procrastinating while negative ingredients continue to blend,
still I await the arrival of the positive spin.

I've seen for years how she's involved deeply in this fight.
I volunteer my assistance,
hoping she will turn these wrongs to rights.

The first step begins with her.
I only wish I knew how hurtful her past issues were.
It's going to be hard work, but eventually she will be less stirred.

The positive spin comes from within.
It's when you make the change in your life and begin,
to see, things as they truly are, not as you want them to be.
Such a reality check…an impact like a train wreck.

Missing or evading the positive spin,
will only keep her fading away from what is real,
like her sanity, and a chance to be whole within.

Sam Davis
12-03-02

We Can Do It

Change what has been going on in your life.
Chances are the past has done you wrong.

Don't be left singing the same old song of
"Sadness."

Happiness will balance the madness.

It's going to be difficult at times to do,
but remember, I am always here for you.
And I will be here forever,
we can fight off what's negative together.

.

Sam Davis
12-06-02

Words

Your words will not hurt me.
They will not stop what I do, or what I try to be.
They are merely words.

You cannot frustrate me by giving me grief.
So well rehearsed by what you might do,
I've prepared beyond your belief.

Keep talking…just keep talking about me,
These, are your insecurities,
and obviously you greatly lack maturity.

So quick to talk about me and judge me,
but you are the only problem as far as I can see.
So again, you just keep on talking,
and I'll just keep walking,
far…far…away from you.

Sam Davis
11-07-02

Which Path?

Standing in the high school hallway smoking a cigarette. Weed in his
pocket,
yellow bandana around his neck, obvious signs, he doesn't get it.

Hanging out at his high school an institution for learning,
being "cool" is his only thought, not a legal dime is he earning.

A negative influence having been influenced negatively,
future days light dim for him as he lives his life aggressively.

Teenaged, confused and hosting rage, obviously not knowing his fate,
but the chariot of death or prison awaits.
Fate never dismisses this notion when one lives with criminal
devotion.

Pissed off at the world, and not knowing why,
he's nearing the end of his tight rope, silently arrives the reality,
he will be jailed, or he will die.

This time is critical in his life. It's totally up to him to decide, he
must fight off the demons of negativity, or be a passenger on that
chariot ride.

Sam Davis
11-17-02

We Rode

For many miles we rode, almost daily,
remember the number of stories we told?

Long term destination unknown.
Speculation doesn't even matter of how many miles we roamed.

College students living in the most natural state.
Searching for knowledge, a time to appreciate.

The laughter so unbelievable as we rode,
so meaningful and inconceivable as now we grow old.

Imagine that, taking the greyhound bus to college.
Too broke to buy a car, yet we constantly thirsted for the knowledge,
necessary to survive in society today.

Look at us now, we've definitely made the grade.

Sam Davis
11-17-02

The Constant Battle

In deep anticipation, I can feel its presence, lurking.
My anxiety level high, I can feel this demon working,
on attacking me. I'm afraid, feeling it has laid low, for now,
perhaps somewhere hiding in the grassy knoll.
I look around cautiously as I search to keep control.

I'm constantly aware of this predator named failure.
Its chilling and haunting stare,
brings on paranoia,
I can feel it's always there.

Hoping to catch me dormant, as its razor sharp teeth
prepare to retract. I move and evade it before it attacks, .
but, at times it does.

I'm injured, in shock from the pain, as its claws pierce my fragile
skin,
trying to force me to give in, constantly telling me that I can't win.

I flee much like the gazelle in the lions grasp.
Mustering all that I have inside, struggling to avoid an energy lapse.
I shake it off and fight it utilizing the strength of my inner will.
I escape finally feeling a bit easier about my wounds,
knowing that with time they will all heal.

Yes failure is the host of my fear.
It is most cruel when it does appear.
So as it continues lurking, I myself will continue working,
on how to avoid it at all costs.

And I vow that as long as I live and my body can hold my breath,
I will fight off the predator failure to the day of my death.

Sam Davis
11-14-02

Just a thought

My mind is scrambled,
 when searching for the correct wording that bests describes you,
  and our existence together.

I am so appreciative because,
 I realize the happiness you have brought,
  into my life.

My life has forever,
 been changed for the better,
  because of you!

I've never thought anyone was,
 worthy of this statement,
  but you are truly too good for words.

That statement fits you,
 and you wear it well.
  I love you sweetheart.

         Sam Davis

Why?

It's so difficult for me to see.
You giving me up, did it set you free?
Was it truly something that had to be?
I only pray you wanted what was best for me.

But why? Is the notion I try to conceive.
I needed your love, why would you leave?
I try and try to understand why. Did I matter to you,
did you tell me goodbye?

Where is my identity? I've never even seen your face.
Did you leave with haste, as you vanished without a trace?
Did you ever think of how I'd feel?
My mass confusion from all that you concealed.
Do I resemble you or do I resemble dad?
Are my lips and eyes like yours,
or are they similar to the ones he had?

For several years you've forced me to ponder,
thoughts like these, as my mind often wanders.
I'm constantly thinking of my own true worth,
all because you abandoned me on the day of my birth.

Sam Davis
10-23-02

Growth

Finally, the morning sun has magically emerged.
My body and soul has finally converged,
signifying a new beginning.

My world has now considerably slowed,
compared to the pace it was spinning.

It has slowed enough for me to get off of it a while,
an attempt at walking a quiet mile.
There is no place for the rapid pace it was twirling.

I'm stable.
I now have in my possession, a mind,
totally free from any depression.
My heart and soul have awakened,
dealing and healing with the beating they've taken.

It appears that my thoughts are now more clear,
making heads and tails of what's been going on here.

My world once again turns, instead of the rapid spinning,
it is evident at this point, I appear to be winning.

Sam Davis
10-25-02

Is this love?

An enchanting passion, so glimmery,
encases my soul. Inside I feel jittery.
Anticipation. In these times I contemplate,
this sensation in which we can both relate.
A longing for another gaze into each other's eyes.

This look, this glance, an innocent hint of romance.
My heart beginning to dance and prance on my soul,
this may be love taking control.

Your aura has taken total control of my emotions and my soul.
I'm immobilized, finding it most inconceivable,
to rationalize if these feelings are even believable.

On the days I see you, do you think of me the way I do you?
I miss those days when you don't show,
I really wish you had let me know.

This phase of my life is new to me. I've never been in love,
but is love truly what I see?

Sam Davis
10-28-02

The Muddy Path

The path my life has taken.
A dirt road at times, quite shaken.
Often times walking this rain muddled path,
finding it difficult to fight off life's wrath.

Yet, I know if not for those days of rain,
I would be helpless to fend off the future pain.
The muddy tracks present, necessary to compensate,
with dues paid, I now know how much I can tolerate.

The muddy tracks represent history.
I can follow them as I backtrack my lifes walk, you see.
Hindsight, so valuable is what I find many times,
it compliments wisdom, at least it does for me.

A man, complete to this day, is how I firmly stand.
Completely full of wisdom and ability,
to see life as it is…total rationality.

Sam Davis
10-01-02

Days

At times, days appear cloudy,
a forecast which may inevitably lead to rain.
A consistent thought pattern hosted inside my mind,
it's these days I feel the most pain.

My mood aligns with this theme.
Dark and cloudy, followed by rain.
My spirit completely in sync with this rhythm,
grasps the feeling of depression and pain.

As the clouds make their exit,
they can reveal the beauty of the sky.
My aura will transform acknowledging this act,
making me joyful, inserting a feeling of high.

Days can be tough to deal with.
The more depressing, the deeper gray your canvas may appear.
Just beyond those gray clouds is a sunny day,
bringing happiness to persevere.

Sam Davis
09-04-02

Taper Street

I've grown up now, and sadly for me
the sun has set on Taper street.
It was the block we grew up on.
A place where young friends would meet.

Growing up in the 70's, a beautiful time, a time that was so sweet.
The watchful eye from every adult, showed us kids love on Taper
street.

My brothers and I would ride our bikes,
together with our friends.
If we were lucky our parents would let us ride down the block,
where Taper street would end.

In a neighborhood which was often times volatile,
and could quickly explode like a bomb.
Taper street was different,
this was one street in the neighborhood that appeared to be most calm.

The countless days we played ball in the street.
The screaming from your parents when it was time to eat.

We played together, and we cried together,
all on this long block.
When the ice cream truck would attempt to pass,
we'd stop it, and like birds, we'd flock.

In the winter, summer, spring, or fall,
in some fashion as a community we would meet.
Such a strong foundation and an appreciation of life,
built for me here on Taper street.

Sam Davis
07-28-02

To Be Me

Told I'm not the same as you,
so much so often.
The thought sits deep inside the mind.
How can I be like you?
I guess the only way to do this,
is to see as you see, do as you do,
be as you be.

Maybe then you will accept me.

But if I do that, I would not be me.
I would be more like you, and I can't be that way.
I must stay, this way,
me,
and proud as can be,
that I am me.

Always staying truthful and real,
to myself,
is the only deal.
Be yourself, and in your heart,
You'll feel the real appeal.

The passage to your destiny.

Sam Davis
07-22-02

Paying Homage to Mom

So dynamic is the
Thought, of the
Way we've been
Taught.

Much like the kindness
In the way we've been raised,
Mom you are an icon,
And should eternally be praised.

It's because of you mom
And your gift from up above,
That we've become adults now,
With the ability to love.

Your will has been imposed
On us in the most positive of ways.
Teaching us to love, is your gift to us forever,
To cherish for the rest of our days.

I love you mom!

Sam Davis
5-20-02

The Correct Path

My destination at one time was unknown.

You came into my life, and we became one.

I don't know how far I would have gone without you,
but I definitely know how far I have come with you.

I am truly complete,
with you at my side.

.

Sam Davis
01-22-02

Slight Confusion

A feeling of emptiness,
Festering deep inside of my soul,
a lack of nourishment,…you know,
having no food inside my bowl.

A foundation unstable,
to say the least,
I'm constantly fighting,
this unchained beast.

This horrible feeling,
That lives inside,
Comes and goes,
Like the ocean's tide.

The worst feeling in the world,
is not knowing where to go,
to fight off these demons, that
are so painful when they show.

They close the walls on me,
From every angle, their presence is so intense,
At times fighting seems so futile,
Rarely making much sense.

So when will it end, and how will it end,
is the question I mostly ask,
how much energy must I use,
to dismiss the awful task.

The demons of abandonment, the demons of trust,
are two of my strongest issues,
but fighting them off requires no comfort,
regardless of the number of tissue.

Often, I look down the road for comfort,
Knowing it's in a close place
Constantly struggling to fight my emotional fires,
And extinguish them without a trace.

This is truly difficult to deal with,
I fight a daily fight,
To correct the weak hand that was dealt to me,
To turn the wrong to right.

Sam Davis 3-15-02

Not what it seemed

I made you feel that
I didn't want your love,
When I honestly cherished
Having it.

I made you feel that
You weren't important
When I honestly new that
You were.

I made you question
If you really wanted to be here with me,
When I honestly would be crushed
If you weren't.

At times sweetheart I have truly
Taken you for granted.
When I honestly worship the
ground you walk on.

Being young and not understanding love
Is why I acted this way.
Because I have honestly loved you
Since day one.

Thanks for being my rock, and being so
Strong, even when I wasn't.
So here's to us,
Our destiny of togetherness with one another.

Sam Davis
5-5-02

ZZZZZ's a coming

Fighting to stay awake this night,
Not wanting my soul exposed.
The sheep assemble at the foot of my bed,
As they leap I began to dose.

I need no doubt to,
Stay awake.
Must try mighty hard,
No matter what it takes.

I sigh and gaze to the clock,
More than wishing it'll stop,
putting a end to the annoying
Tick and tock.

My constant fear is of losing her,
No matter how it seems.
In the day I bury it inside my soul,
Then it surfaces in my dreams.

Lord, please shield me from
This constant nightmare,
you know how hard I've worked,
You know how much I care.

The thought of this is,
So mind blowing.
Can't rest, my mind especially now,
Constantly it's flowing.

Don't want to dream,
Must get this out of my head,
Yet, all I can do is think of her,
And all she's ever said.

I appear to be falling into
A very deep sleep.
The paradox, of having to live this nightmare,
or staying awake and weep.

Sam Davis
2002

From Prince to King

A windy gust of love,
pushed me from behind this morning.
I thought for a second, then let out a sigh.
The presence of my son's resemblance, to me
choked me up, nearly forcing me to cry.

The windy gust also spoke to me, suggesting,
"Hey dad, look at me,"…then he grinned.
His voice quickly called out again.
"I am the mirrors image of you, when you were,
this age, remember?"

A sudden flashback to my youth.

My wife often warned me before his arrival,
that I would react this way. Differently from the arrival,
of his sisters, which of course I love just the same—truly my
princesses.

However, I would have never grown to
become a queen.

I lived my childhood as a young prince, now I live my adulthood,
as a king.

This I can teach him—our eternal bond.

Sam Davis
10-11-01

The Search for Destiny

A short time ago, two souls,
traveled two very different routes.
Both attempted to understand the fate,
of what their lives were truly about.

No matter their travels, the souls would end up,
less than whole and not growing.
Two souls attempting to control their destiny,
trying to conclude where their lives were going.

Destiny—The inevitable fate to which one is destined,
often times is difficult to understand.
We do what we can to control our destiny,
but perhaps that's not in fates plan.

Finally on the same path,
with inevitable luck these two souls would happily meet.
Their destiny once clouded became more clear,
falling in love was the fate they'd greet.

Although a short time ago,
these souls appeared to be solo, somewhat orbiting space,
completeness surfaced much later in life,
they've found their destined place.

Sam Davis
10-25-01

Meant to be

Endless possibilities could have easily landed,
the two of us miles apart from one another.
Yet, here we are together.

At times I have searched high and low,
for my destiny.

I think I have found it, and it's with you.

Sam Davis
10-06-01

Nana

Forever etched in my memory is
the impact you had in my life.

Time has passed and many new memories have,
filled my mind.

Yet, none and I do mean none as important
as when you went away.

Today, another year goes by…It's hard to say that I understand,
because I don't.

My mind stays occupied with life, and all the dealings
that come along with it, but this time of year becomes extremely,
difficult for me to deal with because you,
meant so much to me.

There was so many beautiful days and nights that I spent time,
with you, it would be selfish to continue to be sad,

So I won't.

Because in my mind lives all of those memories of the time spent with you,
and these memories will never escape me. Your energy soars through
me during those thoughts and flashbacks about you

Thank you for being so real, and thank you for making me feel so loved,
and so important.

I loved those times, and I love you.

Samuel Davis Jr.

So, I can say this as unselfishly as I possibly can,

I miss you, Nana.

Mickey
Your 1st grandchild.

Trusting

Deep inside the abyss of my soul,
I search for a reason to TRUST.
Hurt so many times in my past,
these TRUST issues have turned to rust.

I honestly feel that most everyone has,
good and genuine intentions,
but the pain burns profusely from my past,
embracing sanity deserves the most attention.

Untrusting smiles quickly became frowns,
handshakes and hugs became daggers.
I've learned I must abstain from TRUSTING,
and what appears to be a harmless swagger.

Time will expose the frauds.
The pain present, I'm so constantly reminded.
To TRUST again will take much effort,
my eyes wide open, escaping the blindness.

Sam Davis
9-17-01

Challenges

Challenges...
To understand them is to understand,
life.
You will be faced with a variety
of them, count on it, they are inevitable.

For those that have an understanding
of the existence of challenge,
will prosper.

For those that have no comprehension
of the existence of challenge,
will not.

Play the hand of cards that you are dealt,
and deal with these challenges as promptly as
you can. The sooner you do, will allow
you to make room for the next one.

It's right around the corner.

S. Davis

A Little about me

In my world, I would love to be able to trust everyone. That
would be the ultimate satisfaction.

I would love to share my deep rooted and secluded feelings with
a great many.

I want others to tap into every word I speak of.
I want them to explore me emotionally,
climb into my body and walk with me.
See what I've seen, and see what I see.

I want to talk and at times I don't want to listen.

This is why I write. I can declare my thoughts,
showing many of my heart felt emotions, and be heard
loudly without hearing anyone else.

This is my self indulgent departure into my sanctuary.

Young Life Taken Away

I know that you don't know me.
You are clueless to who I am.
I'm just a person that really cares.
I hope you can understand.

My heart feels for your family,
as they try to adjust from day to day,
It's difficult knowing how much they miss you,
although silent, they still have much to say.

Your life maliciously taken forever,
we don't have a clue,
how someone could harm our beautiful children,
specifically, how could they harm you.

You were an angel living here on earth,
that God sent from up above.
I know that you remain with us,
we all can feel your love.

The ending of your life on earth,
is not really an ending.
In heaven your wings spread so much wider,
because of this our hearts are mending.

Watch over your family now,
help them to take the right path.
Help them to forgive the one that took you away,
that person will feel God's wrath.

Fallen

I've asked you several times,
not to place me here.
The strong love that you have for me,
keeping your heart near.

Never needing your physical help,
but always your good advise,
gave me major confidence,
to deal with my life.

You looked at me satisfied,
like I could do no wrong.
And placed me high upon a mantle,
where your heart felt I belonged.

A place unfamiliar to me,
even though you failed to see,
that I am as human as they come.
But you continued to polish me.

You placed me on that pedestal,
and thought that's where I'd stay
But now I've fallen aimlessly,
and may not land today.

I need for you to lift me,
then cleanse me until I shine.
I know I'm only human,
But still I'm one of a kind.

The Magical Things

You're better today, that's quite obvious.
The smile, the hug, the powerful glow.
Your mind has been working very hard,
and your beauty really shows.
It wasn't too long ago,
that the smile, the hug, and the glow were gone.
Being unsure of me, unsure of our love,
you prepared to move on.
I had made some mistakes and have learned from them,
as a man I had to grow.
But through all that time, I cared for you,
If I'd only let you know.
Time has allowed you to understand me,
and you've realized that I've always loved you.
It's taken some time to become a man,
that's what I had to do.
All that time I was so wrong.
Sweetheart I did not know.
How much I missed those magical things,
That hug, that smile, that glow.

For A Short Time

For a short time…

There was no black man, no white man, no militant activists,
no Ku Klux Klan.
Stripped of all of these titles, we began, to work together as a people,
as one we would stand.

Unmentioned were the words Democrat and Republican,
Our political parties had no significance,
and as one we would stand.

We greeted each other with sincerity,
without noticing friendly calm, or the fact it appeared so peaceful.
As a melting pot we were finally one, acknowledging each other as
equals.

Our past issues with each other, truly became past issues.
Past aggressions for a short time disappeared, as did the often lighted
fuse.

The events of September 11, changed America forever and,
for a short time everyone cared for one another.
The sad thing though it took a tradgedy of this magnitude to bring us
together.

But it appears that there is hope for this nation, one day.

Sam Davis
03-29-03

Is It True...

The less hats I wear,
the better off I am?

The odds are better that I will maintain my sanity.

It's definitely a more simplistic method of living.

Sam Davis
03-29-03

It Appears

The less hats I wear,
the better off I am?

The odds are better that I will maintain my sanity.

It's definitely a more simplistic method of living.

But lets be realistic,
as human beings we shy away from what is simplistic.
We delve into what is complex, with total blindness of what to expect.

We make our own lives more difficult,
by the many things we do.
Several activities occupy our time,
knowing that we would be bogged down with few.

It appears that to be human is not to be simplistic.

Many times to be human is not to be realistic.

With so much going on in our lives,
at times we make it so difficult to survive.

It's just that simple.

Sam Davis
03-29-03

Push On

Push on ahead,
regardless of the possibility of failing.
This is my mission.
The key is a clear and positive vision.

My perception,
which is formed through observation,
offers me a bit of understanding,
which assists in my protection.

Like the chess match, I observe before I move.
Observing is my early method of dealing with adversity,
making my life's endeavors a bit more smooth.

But as you know, adversity will find a way to show.
A positive mindset can be helpful in making the adverse process slow.
This key, this positive vision, is all based on what you observe.
Being mindful to the situations of others, the blueprint that,
will help you discover,
what to do,
when adversity comes to visit you.

You must push on ahead.

Sam Davis
03-31-03

At Days End

I look into the mirror preparing to see the usual me.
I didn't recognize this face I saw, it appeared a mystery.

Who was this stranger that gazed back into my eyes?
Was the image I searched for, in danger?
It's been so difficult to live these lies.

"This couldn't be me," my thoughts suggested.
I hoped, but knew that I was wrong.
As years had passed, I was neglectful to see,
the me I had known all along.

This stranger I call a mystery,
was the true image of no one else, but me.
I've suddenly been forced to see my actual face,
discarding the notion of what I wanted it to be,
I appeared out of place.

I guess I'm not the "fairest one of them all."
Harsh realities of what is real,
thanks to my mirror on the wall.
The only way to survive this fall, is to face my mirror,
I guess that's all.

Sam Davis
03-31-03

Strings Attached

The person that constantly works,
hard to satisfy the critics,
is not a person,
but a puppet.
Obviously a puppet
is not a real person,
but a facsimile
there of.

Sam Davis
03-25-03

We

Are we together, or are we apart?
Can indivisible, be divided?
There is no tell all book, no instructions provided.

We as a people are in this together,
whatever endeavor it may be.
We must find a way to get comfortable with "each other,"
then understand that "we means we."

As a people

Drop the titles, and observe,
treat each other in the manner,
they deserve.

All this is important to understanding, the method of "WE."
A word that is wholesome, and is contrary to the word, "me."

Sam Davis
03-31-03

What I Say

I quest to be an individual.
So, I intentionally stray from the societal norm.
My focus is to control and mold my life into its own unique form.

Societal folkways, moreways, discourage
men from revealing their true emotional side.
Disregarding their emotional depth,
confusing what they feel inside, with pride.

I've managed to rebel from this pre-historic method of thinking,
to repel into an arena of modern reality.
A safe haven called honesty, it's truly what encompasses me.

I speak my mind on all levels,
although my sentiments aren't always kind,
you know where you stand with me.
My heart and soul act as my sixth sense, they guide my emotions,
and life becomes less tense.

My heart and soul are filled with love and emotion,
to let pride interfere,
is contrary to my devotion.

Think about this and be real,
it doesn't hurt to allow people to know how you feel.

Sam Davis
03-22-03

Meant to be

Endless possibilities could have easily landed,
the two of us miles apart from one another.
Yet, here we are together.

At times I have searched high and low,
for my destiny.

I think I have found it, and it's with you.

Sam Davis
10-06-01

Sit-In

They set out to change and rearrange, what they knew was wrong.
A mission which came along with many years and many tears.
Hosting bravery, they now feared the ultimate, fighting off a modern
form of slavery.

Praying for the best to past this test of making an impact on society,
but having to react calmly while under fire.
They sat-in together, in places they had been banned seemingly
forever. Yet they constantly strived though being deprived, for what
was right. Passive resistance is how they chose to fight.

"No Negroes allowed," many signs boldly displayed, as this message
weighed heavy on their minds. But how can one find peace in their
mind, knowing they are blatantly being treated unequal, and unkind?

The price to pay was large, not small as they diligently worked to
sacrifice it all. Taking on Jim Crow, and the one's supporting his
laws, willing to give up on living to further our cause.

"Equal treatment," they boldly screamed, and it seemed as if sudden
and fair progress was all they deemed necessary, and it was.

As I walk into a restaurant today, I bow my head and a prayer I'll say
for them. "Thank you," for putting it all out on the line for me. All of
the pain you suffered will not be in vain.

Your struggles have forced me to know, about my past, and how you
fought the laws of Jim Crow, making things better for me, and now
things are even closer to the way they should be.

Sam Davis
11-13-02

Pieces of Me

The many faces of emotionality,
like a puzzle, they assemble me.
They help make me who I am.
It took some time to experience this,
some time to understand.

So many pieces construct my puzzle,
so easy to self-destruct if not careful.
Every situation, every challenge, all I go through,
is all part of me.

Rather good or bad, believe me,
now I see.

A student of life, truly learning,
in a world which sometimes appears so out of control,
such a fast pace, as it's turning.

I understand about these pieces.

Sam Davis
04-02-03

Samuel Davis Jr.

Concluding

I recall my English 1A class while I was attending Humboldt State University. We were on the quarter grading system back then (1985) and that means only nine weeks would pass before grades were final and needed to be submitted. During this class, I diligently attempted to write poetry, but found it very difficult to do. No matter how hard I worked at it, I just could not fit the words and their meanings together. Not long ago I spoke to my mother about this very same issue. My mother (also a published poet) simply responded by saying, "you had not experienced life yet, that is why you found it difficult to write poetry. And this is the reason it comes to you so much easier now, you have experienced a great deal in life." I quickly thought about what she had said and I smiled. She was one hundred percent correct, as usual. Amazing how she continues to offer comfort, wisdom, and understanding to me just as she did when I was a child. But it's true. The poems I presently write are all based on my understanding of life's experiences. These experiences I have now are seen through different eyes as compared to when I was twenty-one years old, sitting in English 1A. My understanding of life is so much more clear.

Life is a roller coaster that we ride during our time here on earth. Some times are good, and others are not. Yet and still, we must make the most of these times, learn from them, and move on to tomorrow. Hence, growth is inevitable if your outlook on life is positive.

I want to thank you all for taking the time to read and digest my material. I hope there is a little of me in you all. Again, this is my 1st book of poetry, but not my last.

Take care.

SD

Samuel Davis Jr.

About the Author

Samuel Davis Jr. was born on October 6, 1964, in Tacoma, Washington. Within months he and his parents moved to Vallejo, California, where his parents had previously lived. He is a husband and a father of three children. He has three brothers and two sisters. Mr. Davis grew up in one of the worst neighborhoods in the city of Vallejo, but because of the guidance of his parents, he managed to attend college, and play college football, where he was a four year starter. He moved to Sacramento, California after attending Humboldt State University in Arcata, California, in 1988. He is a police officer in Sacramento, and has been employed by his department since 1991.

Printed in the United States
16415LVS00005B/541-564